Doggie Data

Pugs

ELIZABETH NOLL

BLACK RABBIT BOOKS

Bolt is published by Black Rabbit Books
P.O. Box 227, Mankato, Minnesota, 56002.
www.blackrabbitbooks.com

Jennifer Besel, editor; Grant Gould, interior designer; Michael Sellner, cover designer; Omay Ayres, photo researcher

Library of Congress Cataloging-in-Publication Data
Names: Noll, Elizabeth, author.
Title: Pugs / by Elizabeth Noll.
Description: Mankato, Minnesota : Black Rabbit Books, [2018] | Series: Bolt. Doggie data | Audience: Ages 9-12. | Audience: Grades 4 to 6. | Includes bibliographical references and index.
Identifiers: LCCN 2016049959 (print) | LCCN 2017003485 (ebook) | ISBN 9781680721553 (library binding) | ISBN 9781680722192 (e-book) | ISBN 9781644661956 (paperback)
Subjects: LCSH: Pug–Juvenile literature.
Classification: LCC SF429.P9 N65 2018 (print) | LCC SF429.P9 (ebook) | DDC 636.76–dc23
LC record available at https://lccn.loc.gov/2016049959

Image Credits

Alamy: Beate Zoellner, 4–5; Bret Edge, 24; Brinkmann, B./juniors@wildlife, 23 (bottom); GROSSEMY VANESSA, 14 (bloodhound); Janet Horton, 22; Juniors Bildarchiv / F314, 10–11; Life on white, 8–9; Naturfoto Online, 17; Nik Goulthorp, 14 (pugs); Phillip Berryman, 18; Tierfotoagentur / J. Hutfluss, 13; Tierfotoagentur / S. Starick, 19 (adolescent); Tierfotoagentur / Traumfoto, 26–27; Dreamstime: Melvinlee, 19 (adult); Shutterstock: Dancestrokes, 28; Eric Isselee, 6–7; Ezzolo, 3, 7, 19 (senior), 20 (top), 32; fongleon356, 12; gp88, 1, Back Cover; kukuruxa, 15 (right); Mac-leod, 15 (left); Sergey Gerashchenko, 23 (top); Timolina, Cover; Utekhina Anna, 31; Vivenstock, 14 (beagle); vutti tangsiripracha, 20 (bottom)

Contents

CHAPTER 1

Meet the Pug

It was a warm day. A boy brought his dog to the park. The boy threw a stick. His little pug ran to fetch it. But the dog wouldn't give the stick back to the boy. The two played a little tug-of-war. Then the pug **sprawled** on the grass. As the dog fell asleep, it farted.

Playful Pups

Pugs are sweet, loving pups. They will follow their owners everywhere. These little dogs like to play. But they tire out easily. Pugs would rather cuddle than run.

How Big Is a Pug?

0
pounds
2
4
6
8
10
12
14
16
18
20
pounds
WEIGHT
14 TO 18
POUNDS
(6 to 8 kilograms)

PARTS OF A PUG

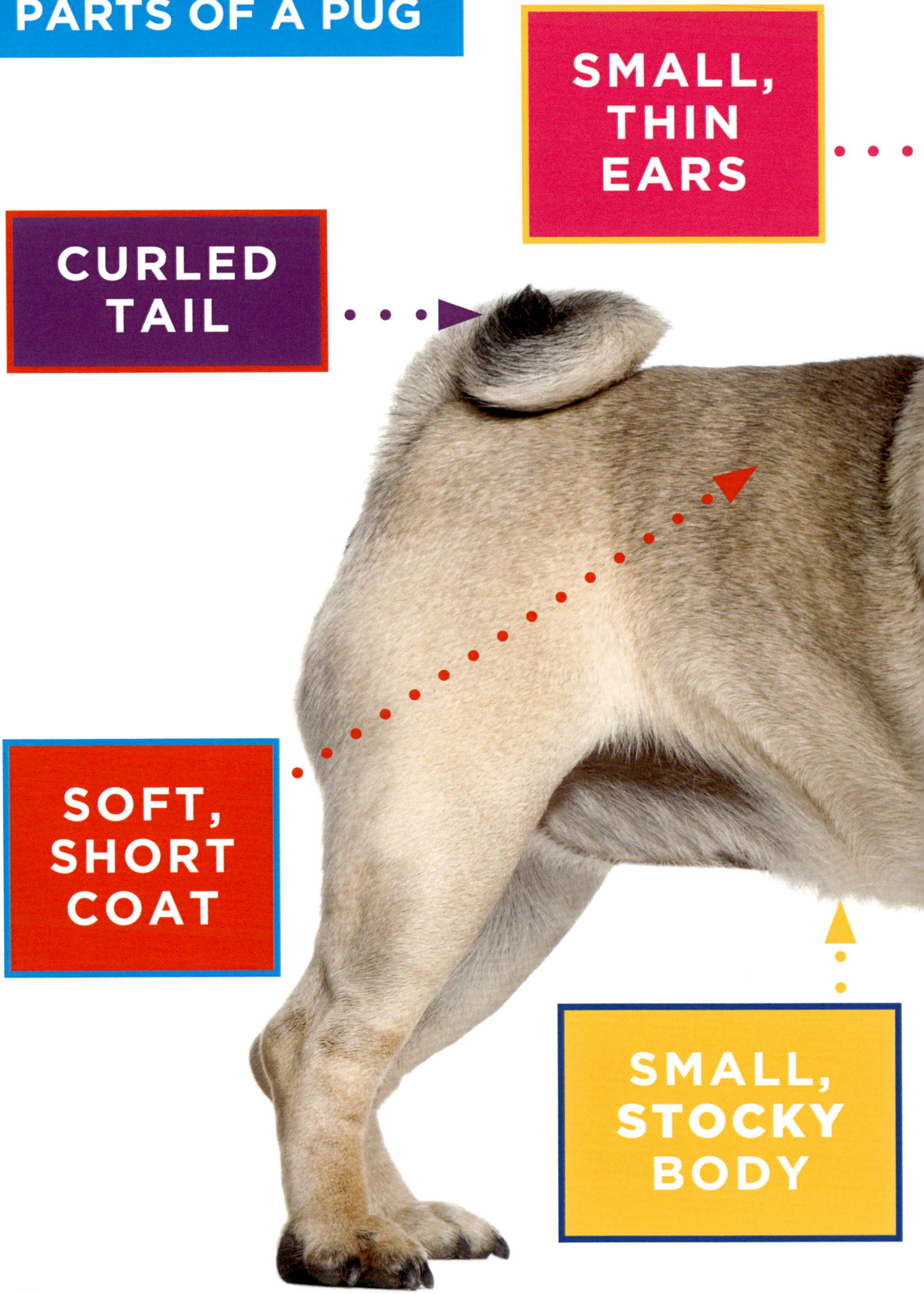

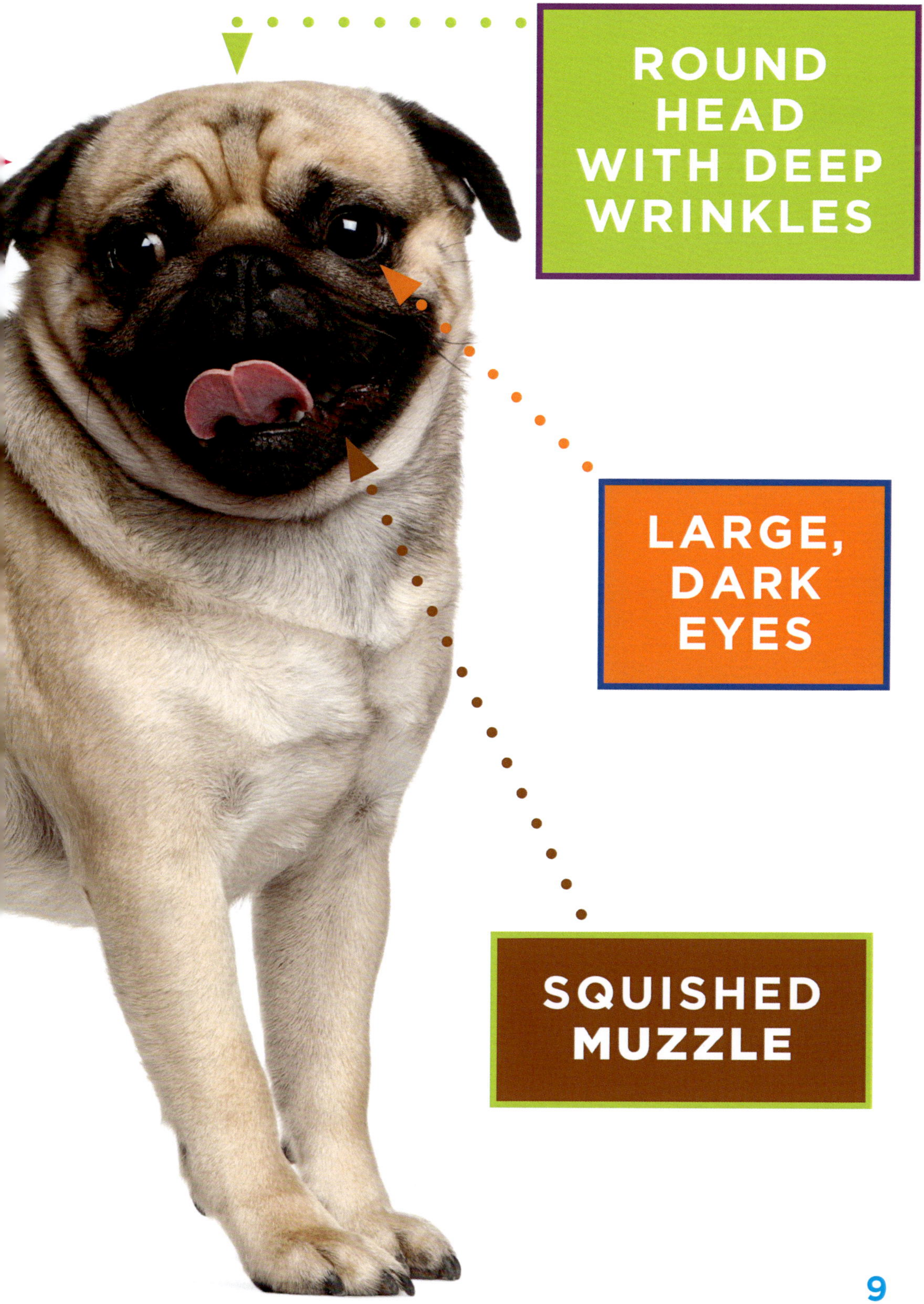
ROUND HEAD WITH DEEP WRINKLES
LARGE, DARK EYES
SQUISHED MUZZLE

CHAPTER 2

A Special Personality

Pugs are happy and **loyal** dogs. They are also clowns. They like to play games and be the center of attention.

These dogs are very smart. But they can also be **stubborn**. With that personality, pugs can be hard to train.

Not Built for Speed

Pugs are curious and funny. But their small bodies aren't built for running. Pugs want to do what their owners are doing. They also enjoy a good nap.

Pugs are a good choice for families that live in apartments.

COMPARING SIZES
BLOODHOUND
80 to 110 POUNDS
(36 to 50 kg)
BEAGLE
18 to 30 POUNDS
(8 to 14 kg)

CHAPTER 3

Pugs' Features

Pugs have big, dark eyes and round faces. Deep wrinkles give them their famous look.

These small dogs only stand about 12 inches (30 cm) tall. Their coats are short too. Their coats can be **apricot**, silver, beige, or black.

Squishy Face

Pugs' faces look pushed in. To many people, this look is cute. But it also causes problems. Their short muzzles cause snoring and wheezing.

All dogs **pant** to cool off. But pugs' bodies don't cool down easily. These dogs often have to pant heavily.

Pugs live about 12 to 15 years.

Pug Life Cycle

Newborn pugs are very sleepy. As they grow, they become more active.

PUPPY

Pugs become seniors at around eight years old. Senior pugs move more slowly and sleep more.

ADOLESCENT

Young pugs are very curious. They lick or bite everything.

ADULT

Pugs are fully grown by the time they're 18 months old.

SENIOR

Pugs were the 34th most popular breed in the United States in 2015.

CHAPTER 4

Caring for Pugs

Like other dogs, pugs need food and water. Veterinarians help owners decide how much food dogs should eat. Pugs like food. Owners need to make sure their dogs don't overeat.

Pugs don't have a lot of energy. They only need about 20 to 30 minutes of exercise a day. These dogs **overheat** if they exercise too much.

Keeping Them Clean

Pugs need some grooming. Their face wrinkles and ears must be kept clean. These dogs shed a lot. So their coats should be brushed weekly. Nails should be trimmed when they get long. Pugs' teeth need brushing regularly too.

Grooming

coat brushing

wrinkle cleaning

tooth brushing

Time and Attention

Pugs need lots of attention. They want to be with their owners. Some people call pugs "shadows." They follow their owners everywhere.

Pugs are known for being gassy. They gulp in lots of air when they eat. Later, it comes out the other end.

Hug a Pug

Pugs are loyal and loving pets. They need lots of attention and daily care. But owners say their pups are worth it.

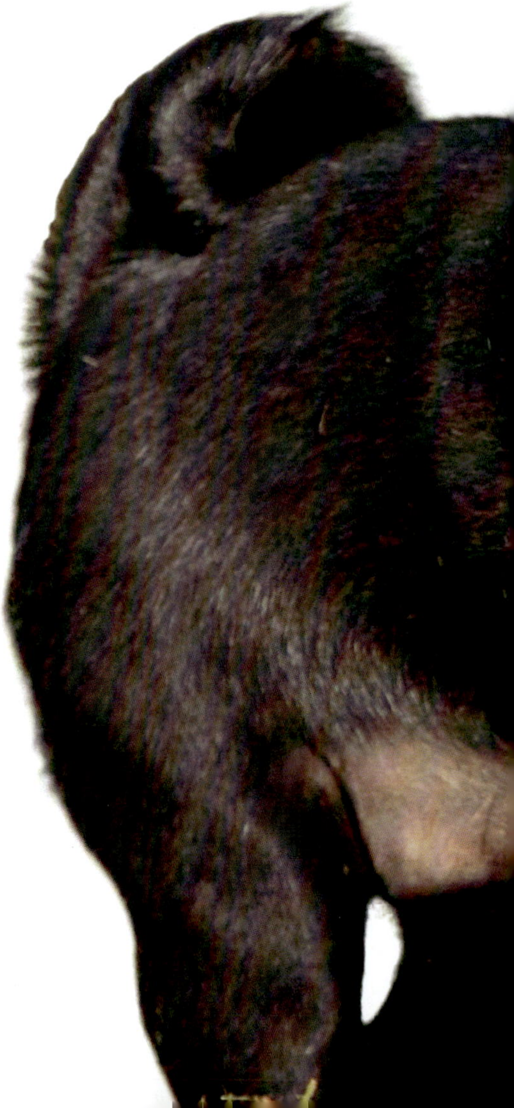

KONG

QUIZ

Is a Pug Right for You?

Answer the questions below. Then add up your points to see if a pug is a good fit.

1 What's your favorite way to spend an hour?

A. playing outside (1 point)

B. baking cookies (2 points)

C. napping (3 points)

2 How do you feel about dog farts?

A. They are so gross! (1 point)

B. I'll just leave the room. (2 points)

C. I fart a lot myself, so they're OK. (3 points)

3 What features do you like best in a dog?

A. sleek and fast (1 point)

B. tough and powerful (2 points)

C. small and cute (3 points)

3 points
A pug is not your perfect match.

4–8 points
You could be a pug's friend. But there might be a better breed for you.

9 points
You and a pug might be great partners!

GLOSSARY

adolescent (ad-oh-LES-uhnt)—a young person or animal that is developing into an adult

apricot (A-pruh-kaht)—an orange color

loyal (LOY-uhl)—having complete support for someone or something

muzzle (MUH-zuhl)—the nose and mouth of an animal

overheat (o-vuhr-HEET)—to become too hot

pant (PANT)—to breathe hard and quickly

sprawl (SPRAWHL)—to lie or sit with arms and legs spread wide apart

stocky (STAH-kee)—short and heavy

stubborn (STUH-bern)—refusing to stop or start doing something

BOOKS

Barnes, Nico. *Pugs.* Dogs. Minneapolis: Abdo Kids, 2015.

Bozzo, Linda. *I Like Pugs!* Discover Dogs with the American Canine Association. New York: Enslow Publishing, 2017.

Gray, Susan H. *Pugs.* All about Dogs. New York: AV2 by Weigl, 2017.

WEBSITES

Pug
www.animalplanet.com/tv-shows/dogs-101/videos/pug/

Pug Dog Breed Information
www.akc.org/dog-breeds/pug/

Pug Dog Club of America
www.pugdogclubofamerica.com

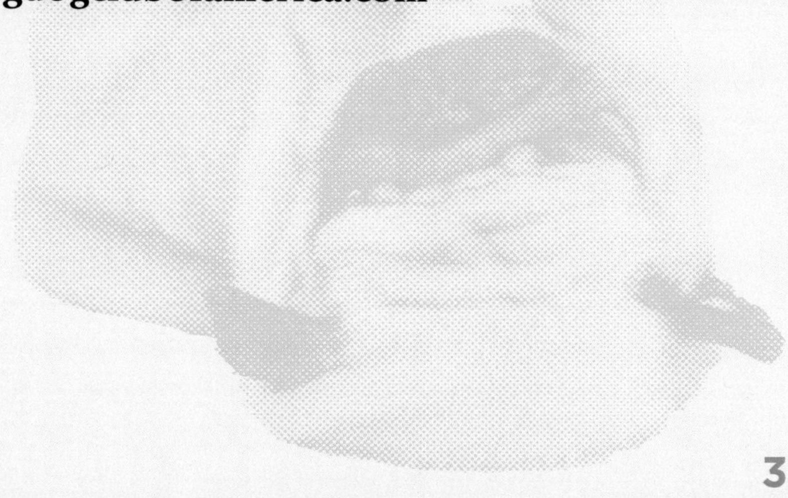

INDEX